If You Can

How Millennials Can Get Rich Slowly

D0950868

WILLIAM J. BERNSTEIN
©2014

ISBN-10: 0-9887803-3-X
ISBN-13: 978-0-9887803-3-0

Front Cover Design by Reality Premedia Services Pvt. Ltd.

Table of Contents

Introduction

Would you believe me if I told you that there's an investment strategy that a seven-year-old could understand, will take you fifteen minutes of work per year, outperform 90 percent of finance professionals in the long run, and make you a millionaire over time?

Well, it is true, and here it is: Start by saving 15 percent of your salary at age 25 into a 401(k) plan, an IRA, or a taxable account (or all three). Put equal amounts of that 15 percent into just three different mutual funds:

- A U.S. total stock market index fund

- An international total stock market index fund

- A U.S. total bond market index fund.

Over time, the three funds will grow at different rates, so once per year you'll adjust their amounts so that they're again equal. (That's the fifteen minutes per year, assuming you've enrolled in an automatic savings plan.)

That's it; *if* you can follow this simple recipe throughout your working career, you will almost certainly beat out most professional investors. More importantly, you'll likely accumulate enough savings to retire comfortably.

But you're still screwed.

Most young people believe that Social Security won't be there for them when they retire, and that this is a major reason why their retirements will not be as comfortable as their parents'. Rest assured that you *will* get Social Security; its imbalances are relatively minor and fixable, and even if nothing is done, which is highly unlikely in view of the program's popularity, you'll still get around three-quarters of your promised benefit.

The *real* reason why you're going to have a crummy retirement is that the conventional "defined benefit" pension plan of your parents' generation, which provided a steady and reliable stream of income for as long as they lived, has gone the way of disco. There's only one person who can repair the gap left by the disappearance of these plans, and you know who that is. Unless you act with purpose and vigor, your retirement options may well range between moving in with your kids and sleeping under a bridge in the rain.

Further, the most important word in this entire booklet is the in the above "if you can follow this simple recipe," because, you see, it's a very, very big *if*.

At first blush, consistently saving 15 percent of your income into three index funds seems easy, but saying that you can become comfortably well-to-do and retire successfully by doing so is the same as saying that you'll get trim and fit by eating less and exercising more. People get fat because they like pizza more than fresh fruit and vegetables and would rather watch Monday night football than go to the gym or jog a few miles. Dieting and investing are both *simple*, but neither is *easy*. (And I should know, since I've been much more successful at the latter than at the former.)

In your parents' day, the traditional pension plan took care of all the hard work and discipline of saving and investing, but in its absence, this responsibility falls on your shoulders. In effect, the traditional pension plan was an investing fat farm that involuntarily limited calorie intake and made participants run five miles per day. Too bad that, except for the luckiest workers, such as corporate executives and military personnel, these plans are disappearing.

Bad things almost inevitably happen to people who try to save and invest for retirement on their own, and if you're going to succeed, you're going to need to avoid them. To be precise, five bad things — hurdles, if you will — must be overcome if you are to succeed and retire successfully:

Hurdle number one: People spend too much money. They decide that they need the newest iPhone, the most fashionable clothes, the fanciest car, or a Cancun vacation. Say you're earning $50,000 per year, 15 percent of which is $7,500, or $625 per month. In this day and age, that's a painfully thin margin of saving, and it can be wiped out simply by stringing together several seemingly innocent expenditures, each of which might nick your savings by $100 or so per month: a latte per day, a too-rich cable package, an apartment that's a little too tony, a dress or pair of brand-name sneakers you really don't need, a few unnecessary restaurant meals and, yes, an excessive smart phone plan you could, if you had to, not only live without, but also function better without. Life without these may seem spartan, but it doesn't compare to being old and poor, which is where you're headed if you can't save. You might even save the whole $625 in one fell swoop just by living with a roommate for a while longer, instead of renting your very own place. Again, as bad as having a roomie may be, it's not nearly as awful as living on cat food at age 70.

Let's assume you *can* save enough. You're not home free, not by a long shot. You've got four more barriers to get by.

Hurdle number two: You'll need an adequate understanding of what finance is all about. Trying to save and invest without a working knowledge of the theory and practice of finance is like learning to fly without grasping the basics of aerodynamics, engine systems, meteorology, and aeronautical risk management. It's possible, but I don't recommend it. I'm not suggesting that you need to get an MBA or even read a big, dull finance textbook. The essence of scientific finance, in fact, is remarkably simple and can be acquired, if you know where to look, pretty easily. (And rest assured, I'll tell you exactly where to find it.)

Hurdle number three: Learning the basics of financial and market *history*. This is not quite the same as the above hurdle; if learning about the theory and practice of finance is akin to studying aeronautics, then studying investing history is akin to reading aircraft accident reports—something every conscientious pilot does. The new investor is usually disoriented and confused by market turbulence and the economic crises that often cause it; this is because he or she does not realize that there's nothing really new under the investment sun. A quote often misattributed to Mark Twain has it that "History doesn't repeat itself, but it does rhyme." This fits finance to a tee. If you don't recognize the landscape, you *will* get lost. Contrariwise, there's nothing more reassuring than being able to say to yourself, "I've seen this movie before (or at least I've read the script), and I know how it ends."

Hurdle number four: Overcoming your biggest enemy—the face in the mirror—is a daunting task. Know thyself. Human beings are simply not designed to manage long-term risks. Over hundreds of thousands of years of human evolution, and over hundreds of millions of years of animal development, we've evolved to think about risk as a short-term phenomenon: the hiss of the snake, the flash of black and yellow stripes in the peripheral vision. We were certainly *not* designed to think about financial risk over its proper time horizon, which is several decades. Know that from time to time you *will* lose large amounts of money in the stock market, but these are usually short-term events—the financial equivalent of the snake and the tiger. The *real* risk you face is that you'll be flattened by modern life's financial elephant: the failure to maintain strict long-term discipline in saving and investing.

Hurdle number five: As an investor, you must recognize the monsters that populate the financial industry. They're very talented chameleons; they don't *look* like monsters; rather, they appear in the guise of a cousin or an old college friend. They are also self-deluded monsters; most "finance professionals" don't even realize that they're moral cripples, since in order to function they've had to tell themselves a story about how they're really helping their customers. But even if they're able to fool others and often themselves as well, make sure they don't fool you.

Only if you can clear all five of these hurdles can you successfully execute the deceptively simple "three fund strategy" I've outlined above.

How can you defeat these five demons? No financial expert, no matter how smart, or how well he or she writes, can tell you exactly how to do this within a few dozen pages of a booklet like this. To torture a metaphor, I can show you the road to Jerusalem, but since the journey takes longer than I have within these relatively few pages, I can't take you all the way there.

In other words, this inexpensive, small booklet is not a taxi cab or an airliner; it's a map.

Acquiring the tools to make you a competent investor will take you at least several months. You can't learn to pilot an airplane in an hour, which is all it'll take for you to finish this booklet, and neither can you become a competent investor in an hour either. The good news is that you're young and in no particular hurry, and that the effort of following the road map will be time well spent.

Now, for full disclosure. First, I've written a few investment books that continue to earn me royalties. I don't want you to buy them, since it's tacky for an author to recommend the purchase of his or her works. I'll shortly tell you what other books you should read, and in what order. Second, I'm also a co-principal in a money management firm. My partner and I specialize in individuals who already have millions; you very well might get there, but I'm old enough that by the time you do, I'll be pushing up the daisies. I am writing this book for my children, my grandchildren, and for the millions of young people who don't have a prayer of retiring successfully unless they take control of their saving and investing.

How to read this booklet

This is, as you can see, a very short booklet and although it will take you very little time to read, you're going to have to read it twice, and the second time will take a while if you do it properly.

After you've completed this booklet, about an hour from now, take another ten minutes and reread the next section, beginning with "Hurdle Number One." At the end of that section, you'll encounter your first reading assignment, which will take you at least a week or two. If you have a busy schedule, it may even take you a month or two.

Then reread the following section, and then complete *its* reading assignment, which again will take you a few weeks or months. And so on, through to the end of the booklet.

This may take you up to a year, but you're in no hurry, since you are just beginning to think about your retirement and you likely have little in the way of assets; you may even be in hock up to your ears with debts from school and car loans. So there's plenty of time, and the months you take to complete the course laid out in the booklet will be the most profitable reading you will ever do; it may not be too much of an exaggeration to suggest, in fact, that your financial life depends on it.

With that out of the way, let's get started.

Hurdle Number One:

Even if you can invest like Warren Buffett, if you can't save, you'll die poor.

How much do you need to save? We'll get into deeper math in the next section, but, as already mentioned, if you're starting to save at age 25 and want to retire at 65, you'll need to put away at least 15% of your salary.

Before you can save, you'll of course have to get yourself out of debt. In thinking about just how to do this, it helps to compare your expected investment return with the interest you're paying on your debt.

Every situation is different, but a few basic principles apply to everyone. First, no matter how much debt you have, always, always max out the employer match on your 401(k), 403, or other defined contribution retirement plan, since the "return" on this money is usually between 50% and 100%, which is higher than even the worst credit card interest rates. (From now on, I'll use the term "401(k)" to refer to any employer-sponsored deferred compensation plan.)

Next, eliminate your credit card debt, followed by your car loan. What about your educational loans? Since your long-term investment return on your retirement savings will be around 5%, which is likely lower than your loan interest rate, you should make paying off those your next priority. When, and only when, you've gotten rid of all your debt are you truly saving for retirement.

The above paragraph raises a subtle but important point about retirement savings. Note that I quoted an "expected return" of 5% for your retirement saving. We'll skip over for now how I arrived at that figure, but for the moment, I'll point out that this 5% number is *not* adjusted for inflation; that is, it is a "nominal" rate of return. I did this so as to more accurately compare it to the loan and credit card interest rates you may be facing.

For the purposes of retirement savings, though, it's better to think about returns that have been adjusted for inflation, that is, "real" rates. Currently, for example, long-term inflation appears to be running at around 2%, so the above 5% expected *nominal* return of your investments calculates out to a 3% *real* return, and what matters is the spending power of your portfolio, that is, its *real* value, not the *nominal* value you'll see on your brokerage or mutual fund statements. From now on, we're only going to talk about real returns and dollar amounts, not nominal returns and dollar amounts; every time you see a dollar figure, you'll have to remember that this is in terms of spending power in the year 2014. One final point: this means that in the above example, planning on saving $625 per month beginning in 2014 means you'll have to increase that savings amount with inflation; this should not be difficult, since you can expect that your salary should increase by at least that rate.

I'll end this section, as I mentioned above, with a reading assignment: Thomas Stanley and William Danko's *The Millionaire Next Door*. This is the most important book you'll ever read, because it emphasizes the point that there's an inverse correlation between spending and saving. (Statisticians and economists like to pooh-pooh this book for its methodological flaws, which admittedly are many. These blemishes, though, in no way detract from the lucid way in which *Millionaire* dissects the corrosive effects of our consumer-oriented society on both personal and societal well being.)

My father was a modestly successful attorney who, because he began his career a few years before the onset of the Depression, became a compulsive saver. Consequently, our house, vacations, and automobiles were not as fancy as those of our neighbors. When I'd ask him why this was, he'd reply that our neighbors *owned* a lot, but didn't *have* a lot. In fact, he'd slyly add, he knew for a fact that more than a few *owed* a lot. (When I was younger, I'd ask him if we were rich: "Your mother and I are comfortably well to do. You don't have a dime.")

Stanley and Danko systematically studied the characteristics of millionaires. Some not-so-surprising facts: the most common millionaire car was an F-150 truck, which offered the most pounds of vehicle per dollar. A plumber making $100,000 per year was far more likely to be a millionaire than an attorney with the same income, because the latter's peer group was far harder to keep up with. And so forth. If this book doesn't scare your spending habits straight, nothing will.

Hurdle Number Two:

Finance isn't rocket science, but you'd better understand it clearly.

Do you know the difference between a stock and a bond? Maybe you do, and maybe you don't, but a little review never hurts.

Say you're starting a business. It'll be a bit before it starts making money, but from day one it'll have expenses, and you'll need money for that up front.

You can get that money in one of two ways: you can borrow it from relatives, friends, or from a bank, or you can sell an ownership interest to a friend or family member. For example, if your brother is half owner, he's entitled to half of all of your business's future earnings.

Nothing prevents you from doing both, and in fact that is what most large corporations do. If you do both borrow money *and* sell shares, then both legally and morally, you have to pay the lenders' interest and principal first. Only after they have been paid, and only after your other ongoing business expenses have been met, can you then pay out the remaining profits to you and your brother.

You and your brother are thus the "residual owners" of the business; if, and only if, you can pay off your lenders and your expenses do you make any money. *From the investors' perspective, an ownership stake (a stock) is much riskier than a loan to your business (a bond), and so the stock deserves a higher expected return than a bond.*

The term "expected return" causes a lot of grief among neophyte investors. It's only what's *expected*, i.e., the average result; the *risk* is the chance that it will fall short. A coin toss that offers a dollar for heads and nothing for tails, for example, has an expected return of fifty cents, but there's also the 50/50 *risk* you'll get nothing.

Here's a good way to think about the relationship between expected return and risk. You'd probably prefer a certain fifty cents for each and every coin flip rather than a 50/50 chance of a dollar or nothing. In fact, most people would prefer even a certain forty cents; only at twenty or thirty cents of certain payoff would the average person prefer the coin flip; this is the point where the higher expected return of the coin flip adequately compensates for the 50 percent chance of getting nothing. (Economists use examples like this to gauge "risk aversion." The person who will not take a penny less than a certain fifty cents to avoid the coin toss has zero risk aversion; the person who will take a certain ten cents to avoid the coin toss is highly risk averse. This paradigm is a good way to think about your own risk aversion—that is, how much risk you can tolerate.)

Put another way, bond ownership has no other upside beyond the full repayment of interest and principal, so it needs to be safe; stocks, on the other hand, need to have their potentially unlimited upside to entice investors who must endure their high risk. Put yet another way, if stocks and bonds were equally risky, no one would own the bond, with its limited upside; conversely, if stocks and bonds had the same return, no one would want to own the stocks, with their higher risk.

This raises a more subtle point, and one that is often not well understood by even sophisticated investors, which is that the interests of the owners of stocks, who are willing to take considerable risks to get higher returns, and the owners of bonds (or, in the case of a small business, the folks loaning it money), who care only about safety, are very different, and it's a company's stock owners who get to vote, not the bond owners. For this reason, loans to businesses — corporate bonds — are in general a bad deal, and it is a good idea to confine your bond holdings to government offerings.

How risky are stocks? You've *no* idea. During the Great Depression, stocks lost, on average, around 90 percent of their value; during the recent financial crisis, they lost almost 60 percent. Although you might think that you can tolerate this kind of loss, guess again. It's one thing to think about temporarily losing 60 percent or even 90 percent of your savings, but the actual experience, in the moment, is unimaginably upsetting. In the words of Fred Schwed, one of the most astute observers of the investment scene (and certainly the funniest):

> There are certain things that cannot be adequately explained to a virgin either by words or pictures. Nor can any description I might offer here even approximate what it feels like to lose a real chunk of money that you used to own.

Is it possible to predict when such declines might occur, and so avoid them? Don't even think about it: in the past 80 years, no one, and I mean no one, has ever done so reliably. Like a broken clock that is right twice a day, many have predicted a single bear market fall, but their future forecasting ability always evaporates, exactly what you'd expect from a lucky guess, and not from skill.

Is it possible to find a mutual fund manager or advisor who can beat the market? Again, no: several decades of careful research have shown that managers with superb prior performance usually fall flat on their faces going forward. (Over the past decade, even Warren Buffett has failed to beat the market by any significant margin.)

The simplest way to think about investing "skill"

is to imagine a stadium containing 10,000 people. Everyone stands up and flips a coin: heads you stay up, tails you sit down. The laws of probability tell us that after 10 coin flips, on average about 10 flippers will still be standing. Were they skillful? Of course not. The poster child for this phenomenon is a money manager named William Miller, whose Legg Mason Value Trust mutual fund beat the S&P 500 index of stocks for *fifteen* straight years before giving back nearly all of his cumulative advantage over that index in just three short years.

Think about it another way. Say you could time the market or successfully pick stocks. Would you be publishing a newsletter, telling people about your predictions on TV, running a mutual fund, or, ha ha, working as a stock broker? Of course not. You'd borrow as much money as you could, bet on your predictions with that borrowed money, and go to the beach. (You might also run a hedge fund, and so direct much of the upside to yourself and all of the downside to your clients.) When all is said and done, there are only two kinds of investors: those who don't know where the market is headed, and those who don't know that they don't know. Then again, there is a third kind: those who know they don't know, but whose livelihoods depend on *appearing* to know.

If you don't find that convincing, think about investing in yet another way: When you buy and sell stocks, the person on the other side of the trade — the person or organization you're buying from or selling to—almost certainly has a name like Goldman Sachs or Fidelity. And that's the *best* case scenario. What's the worst case? Trading with a company insider who knows more about his employer than 99.9999% of the people on the planet. Trading stocks and bonds is like volleying with an invisible tennis opponent. More often than not, that person turns out to be one of the Williams sisters.

If I had to summarize finance in one sentence, it would go something like this: if you want high returns, you're going to occasionally have to endure ferocious losses with equanimity, and if you want safety, you're going to have to endure low returns. At the end of the investing day, only two kinds of assets exist: risky ones (high returns and high risks, namely stocks), and what are known in finance as "riskless" ones (low risks and low returns, like T-bills, CDs, and money market funds). Job one for the investor is to figure out the appropriate mix of the two. For example, the three-fund portfolio presented at the beginning of this book consists of two thirds risky assets and one third riskless assets.

While it's impossible to estimate the returns of the stock or bond markets tomorrow, or even next year, it's actually not too difficult to estimate them in the very long term. First, government bonds. The 30-year U.S. Treasury bond, as of this writing, yields around 3.6%. This is a pretty good estimate of its return over the next 30 years. But this is a nominal return, and recall I just told you that you want to think in real, inflation-adjusted terms. Well, the Treasury also offers a 30-year inflation-protected security (TIPS), that currently has a real 1.4% yield and return of real principal, both of which rise over time with inflation. So the expected real return of the 30-year bond is . . .1.4%.

Stocks are only slightly more complicated. Domestic stocks currently yield a dividend of around 2%, foreign stocks around 3%. This is a *real* yield, since historically the *real* dividend payout increases at around 1.5% per year. Since the stock price should increase roughly in line with this growth in dividends, the real return of stocks should be the sum of the current yield and the growth rate—that is, for domestic stocks, the 2% yield plus the 1.5% growth rate, or 3.5%, and for foreign stocks, about 4.5% (their current 3% dividend plus the 1.5% dividend growth).

Thus, a portfolio that is two thirds stocks and one third bonds *should* have a long-term expected real return of around 3%, and this is also where the suggested 15% savings rate for someone who starts saving at age 25 comes from. Most young people are familiar with Microsoft Excel, so I've uploaded a spreadsheet that shows the effects of varying returns rates and saving rates in terms of real, accumulated assets after 20, 30, and 40 years to www.efficientfrontier.com/files/savings-path.xls. The name of the game is to accumulate around 12 years of living expenses (cells H12 to H16), which, combined with Social Security, should provide for a reasonable retirement. How did I arrive at 12 years of living expenses? The average person needs to accumulate about *twenty-five* years of living expenses, and I'm assuming you'll be getting about half of that from Social Security.

So much for an introduction to basic finance. Your next reading assignment is Jack Bogle's *Common Sense on Mutual Funds*, perhaps the best introduction to basic finance that's ever been written.

I'll end this section with one more bit of full disclosure. I'm proud to call Jack Bogle an acquaintance, but he's also the founder of the Vanguard Group, which is now the world's largest mutual fund company. Four decades ago, he made a fateful decision, which was to give ownership in the company to the *shareholders of the mutual funds*. That is to say, when you own a Vanguard mutual fund, *you* are the owner of the company that offers it. Because Vanguard's shareholders own it, the company has no incentive to gouge them with excessive fees and hidden expenses.

This is the only mutual fund company for which this is true; when you own the shares of any other fund company, you are *not* the owner, and it is in the interest of the company's real owners—the stock shareholders or private owners of the fund company—to keep fees high.

Consequently, Vanguard's fund expenses are generally the lowest in the industry, and the company is my go-to for most investors, whether they have a few thousand dollars or hundreds of millions. I have occasionally been accused of being a "shill" for Vanguard; if wanting to be the owner of my fund company and so pay rock-bottom fees makes me a shill, then I plead guilty.

Jack Bogle, while not a poor man, would almost certainly be a billionaire many times over had he retained ownership in the company, instead of giving it away to the fund shareholders. He is the only person in the history of the financial services industry to have done so and, as you might expect, he has remained, long after his retirement, a strong and clear voice for the rights of small investors everywhere.

Long may he live.

Hurdle Number Three
(with apologies to George Santayana):
Those who ignore financial history are condemned to repeat it.

There is no greater cause of mischief to the small investor than the confusion between the health of the economy and stock returns. It's natural for people to assume that when the economy is in good shape, future stock returns will be high, and vice versa.

The exact opposite is in fact true: market history shows that when there's economic blue sky, future returns are low, and when the economy is on the skids, future returns are high; it is a truism in the market that the best fishing is done in the most stormy waters. In the late 1990s, for example, people thought that the Internet would change everything. It did, but it didn't help the economy that much, and over the next decade stocks suffered not one, but two bone-crushing bear markets that resulted in more than a decade of negative real returns. By contrast, investors who bought stocks in the depths of the Great Depression (and in the depths of the more recent financial crisis) made out like bandits.

By now you know enough investment theory to understand this paradox: since risk and return are inextricably intertwined, high risk and high returns go hand in hand, and so do low risk and low returns. When the economy looks awful, risks seem high, and so stocks must offer high returns to entice people to buy them; contrariwise, when the economy looks great and stocks seem safe, they become more attractive to people, and this yields low future returns. Another way to put it is that the biggest profits are made by buying at the lowest prices, and stocks only get cheap when bad economic news abounds; therefore, the highest returns are earned by buying when the economy is in the toilet, and vice versa.

Learning market history isn't just about knowing the past pattern of returns (though that's helpful). In addition, it's about learning to recognize the market's emotional environment, which also correlates with future returns.

The 1929 market peak offered a classic example of the value of being attuned to sentiment; when asked how he knew to sell stocks the year before, Joseph Kennedy Sr. was said to have answered that when the shoeshine boys started offering him stock tips, he knew it was time to get out. In the 1990s, I had two "shoeshine boy moments." The first came when I saw a TV advertisement for an online brokerage featuring a day trader who had just acquired his own island; the second came when a relative who did not know the first thing about investing joined her first stock club. (One version of the island commercial is available here: http://www.youtube.com/watch?v=1lnwkXb3B-k.) Similarly, you may have observed how during the early 2000s it seemed as though half your friends were flipping houses and brokering real estate and mortgages.

Why the correlation between popular interest and subsequent low returns? Simple: Driving the price of any asset higher requires the entry of new buyers, and when *everyone* is invested in stocks, real estate, or gold, there's no one left to join the party; the entry of naïve, inexperienced investors usually signals the end.

Market bottoms behave the same way; when everyone is afraid of stocks, then there's no one left to sell, so prices are much more likely to move up than down.

Put another way, we often depend on the recommendations of others for, say, restaurants, movies, doctors, or accountants; when all your friends report favorably on one, there's a pretty good chance that the recommendation is valid. Finance, though, for the reasons explained above, is the exact opposite; when all your friends are enthusiastic about stocks (or real estate, or any other investment), perhaps you shouldn't be, and when they respond negatively to your investment strategy, that's likely a good sign.

A working knowledge of market history reinforces this sort of profitable but highly counterintuitive behavior—i.e., to have seen the movie before.

Does the ability to recognize excessive market optimism or pessimism mean that you can "time" the market? No, it does not. Rather, you should use your knowledge of financial history simply as an emotional stabilizer that will keep your portfolio on an even keel and prevent you from going all-in to the market when everyone is euphoric and selling your shares when the world seems to be going to hell in a hand-basket.

Then again, the discipline of maintaining a fixed allocation, such as the 33/33/33 portfolio mentioned at the beginning of the book, is an easy and effective form of market timing, since it of necessity means that you will be buying more stocks after significant market falls, when pessimism reigns, and selling some stocks after prolonged and dramatic price rises, when the market seems to be making everyone rich. The real purpose of learning financial history is to give you the courage to do the selling at high prices and the buying at low ones mandated by the discipline of sticking to a fixed stock/bond allocation.

Section Three's homework is a pair of treats, *Devil Take the Hindmost* by Edward Chancellor, a compendium of stock market manias; and its bookend, *The Great Depression: A Diary*, by Benjamin Roth, a portrait of how things look at the bottom. The lives of most investors encompass the two different kinds of markets described in these books, and they will provide a beacon that will guide you through both the best of times and the worst of times.

Hurdle Number Four

(with apologies to Walt Kelly, creator of the *Pogo* cartoon):

We have met the enemy and he is us.

As you may already have guessed, the person most liable to screw up your retirement portfolio is you. A superb example of just how this happens is found in the March 29, 2013 edition of *Wall Street Journal*, in which reporter Jonathan Cheng described an agreeable, attractive married physician couple, Lucie White and Mark Villa. Wrote Mr. Cheng,

> Feeling "sucker punched," [by the global financial crisis] they swore off stocks and put their remaining money in a bank. This week, as the Dow Jones Industrial Average and Standard & Poor's 500-stock index pushed to record highs, Ms. White and her husband hired a financial adviser and took the plunge back into the market. "What really tipped our hand was to see our cash not doing anything while the S&P was going up," says Ms. White, a 39-year-old

dermatologist in Houston. "We just didn't want to be left on the sidelines."

This story speaks volumes about just how human nature can derail even the best designed portfolio.

In order to understand just how this happens, we need to consider the basics of human evolution. In a state of nature, the biggest risks to human existence tend to be attacks by predators and by other humans, and an ability to react instinctively and quickly carries real survival value. As human beings advanced from agricultural to industrial to postindustrial societies and as health and longevity improved, survival and the quality of life began to depend on a shift to long-run decision making—up to a time horizon of several decades.

Long-term planning, of course, is what investing is all about, and it's a predisposition that our maker most definitely did *not* endow us with. The nearly instantaneous emotional responses that served us so well on the prehistoric African plains turn out to be fatal in finance, as manifested in the buy-high sell-low behavior epitomized by the Villa-Whites.

And that's just for starters. Human nature turns out to be a virtual Petrie dish of financially pathologic behavior. People tend to be comically overconfident: for example, about eighty percent of us believe that we are above average drivers, a logical impossibility. (Men tend to be much worse on this count, and thus worse investors than women.) We tend to extrapolate the recent past indefinitely into the future; in the 1970s, investors thought that inflation would never end, whereas now most people think it will never occur again. The first viewpoint was proven wrong within a few years, and the latter viewpoint most likely will be soon. Both long bear and bull markets also seem to take on a life of their own.

Most importantly of all, humans are "pattern seeking primates" who perceive relationships where in fact none exist. Ninety-five percent of what happens in finance is random noise, yet investors constantly convince themselves that they see patterns in market activity.

Statistics professors use this classic demonstration in introductory courses: the instructor leaves the room and asks all but one of the students to record the results of 30 coin tosses. The one remaining student, chosen by the class without the knowledge of the professor, is asked to *simulate* the tosses with pen and paper.

The professor returns and is able to quickly identify the single student who simulated the coin tosses. How? His or her simulations almost never contain 4 or more straight heads or tails, which almost always occur within 30 *random* coin tosses. The point here is that runs of 4 or more heads or tails are *perceived* as a nonrandom pattern, when in fact they are in fact the rule in random sequences, not the exception. Stock market participants frequently make this mistake, and an entirely bogus field of finance known as "technical analysis" is devoted to finding patterns in random financial data.

Once again, your homework in this section is a real piece of chocolate cake, *Your Money and Your Brain*, by the *Wall Street Journal*'s Jason Zweig; I can guarantee you that you'll enjoy it immensely, and if Jason can't save you from yourself, then no one can.

Hurdle Number Five:

The financial services industry wants to make you poor and stupid.

It's sad but true: by the time you've completed the reading for the previous four hurdles, you'll know more about finance than the average stock broker or financial advisor.

You should avoid them, since their main goal is to transfer your wealth to them. This advice also applies to most mutual fund companies, for the reason mentioned previously: they exist to make profits for their owners, not you.

In fact, the prudent investor treats almost the entirety of the financial industry landscape as an urban-combat zone. To be avoided at all costs are: *any* stock broker or "full-service" brokerage firm; *any* newsletter; *any* advisor who purchases individual securities; *any* hedge fund. *Most* mutual fund companies spew more toxic waste into the investment environment than a third-world refinery. *Most* financial advisors can't invest their way out of a paper bag.

Brokers and advisors may appear to be skilled professionals, but don't be fooled. Doctors, lawyers, and accountants all have the equivalent of post-graduate degrees and had to study for years to pass grueling exams, yet your broker was not required to graduate high school. Further, people do not go into the financial services industry for the same reasons that attract individuals to social work, government service, or elementary education.

Why isn't the public as well protected from mal-feasance in the brokerage industry as it is in medicine, dentistry, accounting, and the law? The reason is that all four of these professions are highly regulated, and their practitioners deviate from standard procedure only at great peril to their livelihood. If a physician fails to recognize and treat with powerful antibiotics more than one or two cases of obvious bacterial pneumonia, his license will get yanked with gusto. Ditto for the accountant or attorney who regularly falls below the standard of practice.

The message of the preceding pages couldn't be clearer; don't come anywhere near a stock broker or a brokerage firm; sooner rather than later you will get fleeced. It's a little known fact that stock brokers do not owe their clients what is known as "fiduciary duty" — the obligation that most other professionals have to put their clients' interests above their own. Without this, you'll have little legal protection from a broker's incompetence and mendacity absent outright fraud or the sale of an outrageously unsuitable investment. (Technically, investment advisors are required to meet a fiduciary standard, but many stock brokers now call themselves "advisors" and are not required to act as fiduciaries.)

Avoiding brokers and advisors is harder than it seems, since they're liable to be your old college roommate, brother-in-law, or church or service organization member. The best way of solving this problem is to deftly change the subject when these folks bring the conversation around to finance or, if you don't mind a little fibbing, to tell them that you have no interest in money management. However you choose to handle this, a ready routine for deflecting approaches from friends and relations in the finance industry is an essential survival skill.

The terrain presented by the mutual fund industry is only slightly less hostile, but because it features greater transparency and the legal protections offered by the 1940 Investment Company Act, it offers you at least a fighting chance of emerging with your wealth intact.

Still, all is not well in the mutual fund world; since fund company revenues flow proportionately from assets under management (AUM), mutual fund companies focus primarily on growing the size of their funds, not on your returns. The good news is that the linkage between these two is far tighter than it is with a brokerage account. Since funds regularly report performance and fees, and since you can so easily move your assets from a fund family's stock fund to your money market fund, from which a check can be written, there is less opportunity for monkey business.

Still, you'll need to exert extreme care with mutual funds. Except for the Vanguard Group, a mutual fund or brokerage company has two sets of masters: the clients who purchase the mutual funds or stocks and bonds in the funds and brokerage accounts, and the shareholders who own the stock of the brokerage or fund company itself. Every company's goal is to maximize the bottom line of the latter — its real owners — and mutual fund and brokerage firms can only do this at the expense of their clients — that is, you. And if you think that your interests are the same as the fund company's — high investment returns — then guess again. By the time you figure out how it's fleecing you, it will have made far more in excessive management fees than it might have made with the higher returns that come from lower expenses. (In other words, if a fund company raises its fund fees from 1.0% to 1.5%, it has just raised its revenues by 50%, but you are unlikely to notice its effect on your performance for many years, if ever.) This same logic applies in spades to brokers, as well, who are very highly trained — in selling, not in finance.

To summarize, you are engaged in a life-and-death struggle with the financial services industry. Every dollar in fees and expenses you pay them comes directly out of your pocket. (Be aware that you're often getting charged far more in mutual fund fees than that "expense ratio" listed on the prospectus or annual report, which is often exceeded by the "transactional costs," that is, adverse price changes that result from moving around millions of shares, much of which accrues indirectly to the fund company.) Act as if every broker, insurance salesman, mutual fund salesperson, and financial advisor you encounter is a hardened criminal, and stick to low-cost index funds, and you'll do just fine.

Now for the good news: you've already done the homework for this section, which is the same as for Section Two, *Common Sense on Mutual Funds.* So you've almost finished the reading list.

What about the nuts and bolts?

So, how do you actually implement the investment plan outlined above? As mentioned in the first section, your biggest priority is to get yourself out of debt; until that point, the only investing you should be doing is with the minimum 401(k) or other defined contribution savings required to "max out" your employer match; beyond that, you should earmark every spare penny to eliminating your student and consumer debt.

Next, you'll need an emergency fund placed in T-bills, CDs, or money market accounts; this should be enough for six months of living expenses, and should be in a taxable account. (Putting your emergency money in a 401(k) or IRA is a terrible idea, since if you need it, you'll almost certainly have to pay a substantial tax penalty to get it out.)

Then, and only then, can you start to save seriously for retirement. For most young people, this will mean some mix of an employer-based plan, such as a 401(k), individual IRA accounts, and taxable accounts.

There are two kinds of IRA accounts: traditional

and Roth. The main difference between the two comes when you pay taxes on them; with a traditional account, you get a tax deduction on the contributions, and pay taxes when the money is withdrawn, generally after age 59½. (You can withdraw money before 59½, but, with a few important exceptions, you'll pay a substantial tax penalty for doing so.) With a Roth, it's the opposite: you contribute with money you've already paid taxes on, but pay no taxes on withdrawals in retirement.

There's thus not a lot of difference between a 401(k) and a traditional IRA; in fact, you can seamlessly roll the former into the latter after you leave your employer. In general, the Roth is a better deal than a traditional IRA, since not only can you contribute "more" to the Roth (since $5,500 — the current annual contribution limit — of after-tax dollars is worth a lot more than $5,500 in pre-tax dollars), but also you're hopefully in a higher tax bracket when you retire.

Your goal, as mentioned, is to save at least 15 percent of your salary in some combination of 401(k)/IRA/taxable savings. But in reality, the best strategy is to save as much as you can, and don't stop doing so until the day you die.

The optimal strategy for most young people is thus to first max out their 401(k) match, then contribute the maximum to a Roth IRA (assuming they're not making too much money to qualify for the Roth, approximately $200,000 for a married couple and $120,000 for a single person), then save in a taxable account on top of that.

A frequent problem with 401(k) plans is the quality of the fund offerings. You should look carefully at the fund expenses offered in your employer's plan. If its expense ratios are in general more than 1.0%, then you have a lousy one, and you should contribute only up to the match. If its expenses are in general lower than 0.5%, and particularly if it includes Vanguard's index funds or Fidelity's Spartan-class funds (which have fees as low as Vanguard's), then you might consider making significant voluntary contributions in excess of the match limits. For most young savers, fully maxing out voluntary 401(k) contributions (assuming you have a "good" 401(k) with low expenses) and the annual Roth limit will get them well over the 15 percent savings target.

Your contributions to your 401(k), IRA, and taxable accounts should be made equally to the indexed U.S. stock, foreign stock, and bond funds available to you. Once per year, you should "rebalance" them back to equal status. In the good years, this will mean selling some stocks, which you should avoid doing in a taxable account, since this will incur capital gains taxes. In practice, this means keeping a fair amount of your stock holdings in a tax sheltered 401(k) or IRA. This will not be a problem for the typical young investor, since he or she will have a relatively small amount of his or her assets in a taxable account.

The following are some examples of the kinds of index funds you'll want to use. If your 401(k) is lucky enough to have Vanguard funds, look for, respectively, the (U.S.) Total Stock Market Index Fund, Total International Stock Index Fund, and either the Short-Term Bond Index or Total Bond Market Index Fund. As already mentioned, the Fidelity Spartan series is also excellent: the Total Market Index, International Index, and U.S. Bond Index (or Short-Term Treasury Bond Index) funds.

Increasingly, 401(k) plans are making "target funds" the default contribution choice. For example, Vanguard offers Target Retirement funds, which carry fees of 0.16%–0.18%, aimed at those retiring between 2010 (geezers) and 2060 (twenty-year olds) in 5-year increments (2060, 2055, 2050, and so forth, down to 2010). The 2060 fund, for example, has a 90% allocation to stocks, which will then fall by a percent or so each year as the saver gets older.

This is about as far as I can take you in this book with the nuts and bolts. There's nothing magic about a portfolio consisting of equal parts U.S. stocks, foreign stocks, and bonds; you might want a higher or lower allocation to each of these, and you might even want to "slice and dice" the U.S. and foreign stock components into smaller component pieces such as real estate investment trusts (REITs), emerging and developed markets for foreign stocks, and so forth. And, as I've said, there's nothing wrong with an all-in-one target retirement fund, as long as it has low expenses.

Since Section Five had no homework assignment, I'm going to double up the reading assignment with two books: Allan Roth's *How a Second Grader Beats Wall Street* and Rick Ferri's *All About Asset Allocation*.

That's it. As I told you in the beginning, if you've completed your first pass through the booklet, take a deep breath and start with the Section One reading assignment, *The Millionaire Next Door*, then continue with the rest.

There are a number of things I haven't told you, the most important of which is how to spend down your money in retirement. At present, the best way of doing this is the purchase of an inflation-adjusted fixed annuity, which mimics the payout of a traditional pension plan, or a "ladder" of inflation-protected bonds (TIPS) that matures every few years, to provide you with an inflation-adjusted income stream. Estate planning is another issue I haven't discussed, since it's even further out in the future.

The reason I haven't talked about either retirement spending or estate planning is that both will not become important to you for many decades, by which point the relevant investment options and tax law will almost certainly be very different from today's. So it's just not worth thinking about these two issues now. In other words, you're way too young for these things to matter, for the simple reason that they'll be very different by the time they do.

Back to the present; if this is the end of your second pass through the booklet, and you have thus completed all of the sectional reading lists, then you're ready to start on your journey to a reasonably well-to-do retirement.

Good fortune!

William J. Bernstein
Portland, OR
March 2014

Made in the USA
Las Vegas, NV
02 January 2022

40106965R00028